VIRTUE STORIES

When in doubt, tell the Truth

Lalita Iyer

Om KIDZ
An imprint of Om Books International

Matt came home from school, threw his satchel, gulped his smoothie and was ready to dash off to play.

'You seem really eager to go out and play these days,' said his mom.

She was right. Matt had made a new friend, Joe, in the apartment block. The fact was that more than playing football with him, which they did, Matt loved listening to Joe's stories about the X box games he played at home. Joe was eleven, four years older than Matt, and Matt loved that an older, much taller boy enjoyed playing with him. It made him feel very special.

That day, after kicking around a bit, Joe casually asked, 'Want to come to my place and play a shooting game? There is no one at home.'

Matt knew that he wasn't allowed.

'But… but… my mom says…'

'There's no need to tell your mom. No one will know. Come for a bit?'

Tempted, Matt went along. He knew mom would be furious if she came to know. He wasn't allowed to play video games or to go to anyone's house without her permission. He went, anyway.

When they reached the house, he was secretly happy Joe's mother was not at home. 'Let's do double player,' he said, handing Joe a controller and encouraged him. 'Go for it!'

There was a lot of shooting in the game but Matt kept shooting the wrong guys and Joe kept getting annoyed at him. Finally he said, 'Okay, may be you just sit there and watch me,' taking back the controller from Matt.

For the next hour, Joe also stopped talking to him and soon, Matt had a headache because of the noisy gunfire, but he said nothing. He felt like crying but what could he do?

After a brief silence, he quietly got up and went home and began to do his homework. Joe barely said bye to him when he left.

When his mother entered his room, she was surprised. 'You are here? I thought I'll pick you up from the football ground, but I couldn't find you.'

'Oh…I …I…'Matt muttered uncomfortably, wondering what to say.

'You decided to come home early and do your homework and please your mamma?' she said. 'What a good boy you are!'

Matt was confused. His mom trusted him so much! He could have easily got away with it this time. But something bothered him inside about hiding stuff from her.

'Actually mamma, I did something you won't approve.'

'Really? What?'

'Well, I went to play X box at Joe's house, but I didn't like it, so I came home.' Matt's mother was really shaken.

She wondered. Is he in bad company? Should I be worried? What if he ends up playing some violent games? How dangerous is this? A thousand thoughts rushed through her mind. But she decided to stay calm.

Matt, after all, had spoken the truth when he could have easily got away with not telling her.

‘I am glad you told me, Matt. I really appreciate your honesty,’ she said hugging him tightly.

As she put her things away, she added, 'Maybe I could download some non-shooting games for you on my iPad and you could play for half-an-hour every day after homework. How does that sound?

Matt couldn't believe his ears! So, speaking the truth had some rewards after all!